Mulvoy, Mark
   Sports Illustrated curling: techniques
and strategy, by Mark Mulvoy with Ernie
Richardson. Photos. by Donald Newlands.
Lipponcott, c1973.
   107 p. (The Sports Illustrated library)

   1.Curling. I.Richardson, Ernie. II.
Sports Illustrated (Chicago). III.t.

Sports Illustrated

CURLING:
Techniques
and Strategy

The Sports Illustrated Library

Sports Illustrated
CURLING:
Techniques
and Strategy

BY MARK MULVOY
WITH ERNIE RICHARDSON

Photographs by
Donald Newlands

J. B. LIPPINCOTT COMPANY
Philadelphia and New York

U.S. Library of Congress Cataloging in Publication Data

Mulvoy, Mark.
    Sports illustrated curling: techniques and strategy
(The Sports illustrated library)
    1. Curling.   I. Richardson, Ernie.   II. Sports
illustrated (Chicago)   III. Title.
GV845.M84 1973   796.9′6   73–3487
ISBN–0–397–00832–5
ISBN–0–397–00816–3 (pbk.)

Copyright © 1973 Time, Inc.

Printed in the United States of America

Contents

Sports Illustrated
CURLING:
Techniques
and Strategy

1
Introduction

ALTHOUGH curling is played on ice and golf is played on grass, there is, oddly enough, a similarity between the two games. For one thing, historians and other experts trace the beginnings of both sports to Scotland. Unfortunately, curling does not have its St. Andrew's. Indeed, every loch in Scotland probably can claim that the first rock ever curled was skimmed over its frozen surface on a cold, crusty morning way-back-when. Finding themselves without a leisure-time activity once the weather conditions turned too mean for golf, the inventive Scots discovered the game of curling.

They dislodged large, smooth stones from the river beds and the coastal shores and used them as their rocks. There were no formal rules then; the rocks were thrown down the ice for pleasure. For the strong, burly Scots, there were distance contests: How far could they slide their rocks across the ice? For other Scotsmen, there were accuracy contests: Who could skim his rock through the opening between those two sticks across the ice? Later, as more and more people took up the game, it developed into the refined sport that it is today. It became a game demanding both accuracy and strength.

Curling is a very simple yet very complex game. It is not a

game of chance, not a sport of luck. It requires mental alertness even more than any purely physical quality. Curling is controlled action—a game of intricate maneuvers, delicate shots, accuracy and physical conditioning. An out-of-shape man or woman cannot handle a 40-pound stone and direct it at a target some 120 feet away. Not for very long, anyway.

GLOSSARY OF CURLING TERMS

Like all sports, curling has a language of its own. What a no-hit inning is to baseball, a blank end is to curling. What the cup or the hole is to golf, the button is to curling. Here is a basic curler's glossary.

BITER. A rock that barely touches the 12-foot, or outermost, ring.

BLANK END. A scoreless end.

BONSPIEL. A series of curling competitions with many different events.

BURNED ROCK. A moving rock accidentally touched by a sweeper's broom. A burned rock is immediately removed from play.

BUTTON. The area inside the rings in the house.

CENTER LINE. A line drawn between the hack and hog line at a distance of 7 feet from either side of the sheet, passing through the tee line at the center of the button.

CHAP AND LIE. A strategy whereby the skip instructs one of his players to have his rock take out an opposition rock and keep his own rock inside the house.

CHIP. A rock that barely touches the edge of another rock.

CIRCLES. The four rings at both ends of the ice to which all rocks are directed. Also known as the house.

CLOSE A PORT. To block any opening between two stones in the house.

COUNTER. The rock closest to the center of the house.

DRAW. To deliver a stone so that it will stop somewhere inside the house.

DRAW WEIGHT. The force needed on a rock to make it reach the house.

END. Curling's version of an inning, a quarter, a period, a hole. An end is over when all eight curlers on the two teams have shot two rocks apiece. There can be eight, ten or twelve ends in a game.

FREEZE. Two stationary stones touching each other, with one stone in front of the other.

GUARD. A stone that protects another stone from being taken out of play by a third stone.

GUARD WEIGHT. The amount of force needed on a rock to place it in front of the rings and protect a rock in the house.

HACKS. The starting blocks, or foot supports, at the two ends of the ice from which all players begin their slide. Right-handed players use the right hack; left-handed curlers, the left one.

HEAD. The four rings, also called the *house* and the *circles*, toward which the rocks are directed.

HEAVY. More weight on a rock delivered by a player than the skip intended.

HEAVY ICE. Bad ice, caused by too much water, too much frost or too much pebble, that causes the skip to call for heavier rocks from his players.

HITTING WEIGHT. The amount of force needed on a rock to make it push a rival rock out of the house.

HOG LINES. Two lines—one at each end of the rink—33 feet in front of the hacks. Players cannot slide past their own hog line on their followthrough, and their stones must pass the hog line at the other end in order to remain in play.

HOUSE. The four rings (circles or head) toward which the rocks are directed.

IN-TURN. A moving stone, the handle of which turns clockwise.

LEAD. The first player to curl in an end.

LIGHT. A rock delivered by a player that has less weight than the skip intended.

NARROW. The delivery of a rock inside the spot indicated by the skip with his broom.

OUT-TURN. A moving stone, the handle of which turns counter-clockwise.

PEBBLE. Water frozen to form a surface of many bubbles.

POCKET. A group of rocks resting in a semicircle, concentric with the circles and almost always behind the tee line.

PORT. An aperture between two rocks that permits the passage of another rock.

PULL. The change in course of a rock as it slides down the ice.

RAISE. To hit a rock and move it closer to the tee line.

RINK. A team of curlers. Also the building in which curling is played.

ROLL. The movement of a rock after it has struck another rock.

RUB. To barely touch another rock while passing it.

RUN. A tricky place on the surface of the ice that alters the course of the sliding rocks.

RUNNER. A stone traveling very fast.

SECOND. The player who follows the lead in an end, after the rival lead has played his shots.

SHEET. The ice surface on which the game of curling is played.

SHOT ROCK. The stone lying closest to the tee line.

SKIP. The last player to shoot on a team; he calls the strategy for the other three players.

SLIDE. The natural followthrough after a curler delivers his rock.

SWEEP. To clean the ice in front of a rock with a broom to add distance to its slide.

TAKE-OUT. Removal of a rival rock from play by striking it with your own rock.

TAP WEIGHT. The amount of force needed on a rock to make it nudge a rival rock out of position or curl around short guards.

TEE LINES. The two lines, 114 feet apart, drawn from side to side through the buttons, at right angles to the center line.

THIRD. Also known as the vice-skip, the third man on a team to deliver a rock.

VICE-SKIP. See *Third*, above.

WEIGHT. The amount of force or momentum on a stone as it moves down the ice.

WICK. To strike the edge of another rock.

14

WIDE. The delivery of a rock outside the spot the skip indicated with his broom.

WOBBLER. A fast-moving stone that wobbles along down the ice. Curling's answer to the knuckleball.

WRECKED SHOT. A stone that accidentally wicks off a rock in front of the house.

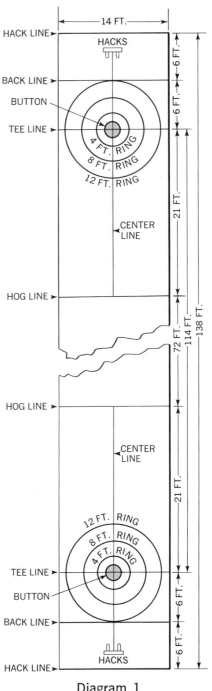

Diagram 1

2
The Game of Curling

THE SHEET OF ICE

Curling is played in a rink that is divided into numbered "sheets" of ice (similar to bowling alleys or lanes). Diagram 1 gives the dimensions and identifies the essential parts of a sheet.

THE GAME

Curling is played by two teams, or rinks, consisting of four players each. Each one delivers two stones down the sheet of ice, starting from the hack line at one end and directing them to the house some 125 feet away. The interval during which all sixteen stones are delivered is called an end, and the object is to complete each end with your rocks closer to the center of the house than your opponent does. Normally, there are ten ends in a game, but there can be eight or twelve, depending upon the competition being played.

Part of the strategy of the game involves the placement of your own rocks; part involves moving your opponent's rocks out

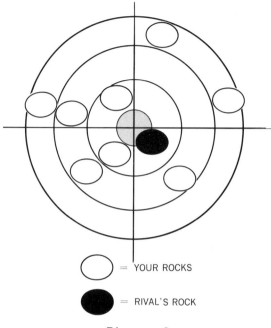

= YOUR ROCKS

= RIVAL'S ROCK

Diagram 2

of scoring position. At the finish of each end, the team with the rock closest to the button scores 1 point, and then scores an additional point for every rock nearer the button than the closest rock played by the rival team.

Confusing? Then consider the situation depicted in Diagram 2.

You have all eight of your rocks in the house while your opponent has only one. However, his rock is closer to the button than any of yours; therefore he scores 1 point and you are shut out. On the other hand, if all eight of your rocks were closer to the button than his single rock, you would score 8 points—the maximum for any one end. Eight-point ends, though, happen about as often as it snows in Miami, Florida.

The team that wins the toss-up plays its rocks last. Thereafter, the team that does not score in one end has last-rock advantage. As you can understand, the last rock shot in an end is most important, since it usually determines the outcome of that end.

If the skip—who plots the strategy for a team—has last-rock advantage, he can do any number of things with his final rock, depending upon where the other fifteen rocks are. He can take out a rival rock if it is nearest to the button. He can play for the button himself. Or he can play through the house and preserve the last-rock advantage for the next end.

Stated simply, the skip is the quarterback for his rink. But unlike football, in curling the skip does not study films of the opposition and formulate a game plan beforehand. Once a game begins, though, a good skip should be able to detect the strong points and the weak points of the rival players. If they are not good at the draw game, the skip should know it. If there is no particularly strong take-out man, the skip should know that. By recognizing what his rivals can and cannot do with their rocks, and also by studying the ice surface, the skip can prepare a winning plan of attack for the match. He stands in the house until his turn comes, and signals his players where he wants their rocks placed.

The first four rocks are delivered by the *leads* on the two teams, playing alternately. Next to play are the two *seconds*, followed by the *thirds*, or *vice-skips*. The two skips are the last to deliver their rocks.

All four members of a team can sweep the ice after a rock has been released, but the main sweepers are the lead and the second until the stone reaches the tee line. Sweepers are very important in a curling game, for they help determine the speed and the direction of the rock as it moves into or out of the scoring area. Good sweeping, for instance, can affect the length of a throw by as much as 10 or 15 feet on keen ice. Sweepers cannot touch a moving rock. If they do, the rock is removed from play.

Curling is an art that demands constant practice and a totally unselfish attitude. It is a game where teams, not individuals, win. Discord and selfishness breed defeat in curling, just as they do in all other team sports. Remember what Joe Kapp once said about football? "Eleven for one." Well, in curling it's "Four for one"—or else. The four best curlers in the world would form

19

the worst team in the world if they permitted their personal vanities to get the best of them. Indeed, when the Richardsons of Regina, Saskatchewan, Canada, were dominating the world's curling teams back in the late 1950's and the early 1960's, they were the perfect blend of ability and attitude.

THE RULES

Curling has not only its formal rules of play but also its rules of etiquette. Indeed, it is one of the few sports in the world that emphasizes etiquette. Golf, of course, is another. But can you imagine a football lineman moving aside to let a ballcarrier pass? Or a second baseman running away from a ground ball in order not to interfere with the base runner? Or a hockey defenseman letting a shooter remain on his feet after releasing the puck? Hardly. But then, curling—like golf—is not a game of physical contact.

Some Important Rules of Play

1. A sweeper cannot touch a moving stone with his broom or his body. If he does, the stone must be removed from the ice.

2. Disputed shots must be settled by the vice-skips, an umpire or a neutral party, in that order. Only an umpire can measure a stone before the conclusion of an end, and even then he can decide only whether or not a stone is "alive."

3. A stone is out of play, or "dead," once it crosses the back line.

4. A stone must pass the far hog line in order to stay in play, or alive, unless it strikes another stone first.

5. If any member of the rink is missing, the lead must play the missing person's stones. When the lead is missing, the second must play the extra stones.

6. Players must start their delivery from the hack, but they cannot let any part of their body or broom pass beyond the near hog line during the delivery. If that happens, the stone must be removed from the ice.

7. Only the skips and the vice-skips can sweep beyond the tee line.

8. Only the skips and/or the vice-skips can remain within the house during play, with the skip or vice-skip of the playing team having his choice of position.

9. If a stone turns over or finishes on its side or top, it, too, must be removed from the ice.

10. A stone must touch the outer 12-foot circle to be eligible for scoring.

Some Important Rules of Etiquette

1. Do not be near the center of the ice while a stone is in motion if you are not sweeping. Inactive players should stand along the sides of the sheet, well out of play.

2. Never disturb a curler when he is in the hack. Keep your distance and be silent and motionless.

3. Be ready to throw your stone when your turn comes. And don't dawdle in the hack. Slow curlers invariably are bad curlers, for it is impossible to maintain mental readiness for too great a period of time when you are holding a 40-pound rock in your hand.

4. Don't walk or run across the ice when a rival player is in the hack or studying his shot or when a rival stone is in motion.

5. Don't run to the lounge for refreshments between shots. Instead, stay around, encourage your teammates and try to learn something about your rivals.

6. Never discuss curling technique with a teammate or a rival player during a game. While "talking an opponent out of a shot" may be part of a golfer's psychology, it has no place in curling.

7. Don't lose your temper.

THE EQUIPMENT

The curler, unlike the golfer, needs very little in the way of equipment in order to enjoy himself for a few hours or an entire season. For a golfer, there's $400 for a set of clubs, at least that much money for a wardrobe and about $2,500 a year for his country club membership. The curler's expenses, on the other hand, are much less. Curling clubs provide the ice and the hacks.

The curler himself needs very little. For years curlers have worn heavy knit sweaters. Rinks generally wear the same matching sweaters every year, complete with patches or other markings that help identify them as, say, the Richardson Rink. Sweaters tend to be very colorful and certainly add an extra dimension to the game. Most curlers wear gloves too. Some need them during delivery to stop their forward motion short of the near hog line after a long slide. Ernie Richardson recommends a pair of thin gloves for all curlers to keep their hands warm and yet maintain a "feel" for their rocks. He uses deerskin gloves with padding, mostly because he has a tendency to develop blisters on his hands. All clothing should be loose-fitting enough to be comfortable.

In recent years the "in" thing in curling has been special curling boots, but they are not entirely necessary for the average curler. The new-style boots have a so-called "slider"—a hard, smooth finish—on the bottom of the left boot (or right boot for left-handed curlers) and supposedly make the trip from the hack to the hog line much easier on the feet and on the ice. Some curlers wear a separate "slider" over the shoe of the sliding foot.

The Broom

Each curler has his own broom. The broom is to the curler what a putter is to the golfer. It is his, and he has a feel for it. Not surprisingly, brooms—like curlers' sweaters—have become decorative over the years, if you can imagine a broom being decorative. The best curling brooms are made from corn bloom and have fairly narrow, tapered bottoms, and all have so-called "skirts" around them. Why? Mainly for looks. But the skirt does cover up the cording that binds the corn bloom. While some curlers have changed to a spongelike foam covered with wool, the basic corn-bloom broom still is the best sweeping device for the curler. Selection of the broom should depend on the curler's size and weight. He must be able to maintain good leverage and have a strong, fast stroke.

The Stones

Stones, though, are not a personal matter. Imagine, for one moment, Jack Nicklaus teeing off in the United States Open with Arnold Palmer's driver, Bobby Orr shooting pucks with Bobby Hull's stick, Rod Laver serving tennis balls with Ken Rosewall's racket and Maury Wills swinging Harmon Killebrew's baseball bat. Of course not. But curlers think nothing of using their teammates' stones and, in fact, few have what might be called their private stones. Most clubs nowadays provide matched sets of stones for their members. In the old days, rocks used to weigh between 36 and 42 pounds, depending on the preference of the individual curler, so most curlers had their own. But with the stones now standardized at 40 pounds, and with all the handles identical (except for color), there is no longer a need for curlers to own them.

A curler's stone looks something like a tea kettle. On both top and bottom of the stone there is a cup with a small sliding edge. When one edge wears down, after about 5 years, the ice maker simply turns the stone over and installs the handle on the other side; the stone is then used until that edge wears down. When both sides have worn down, the rink manager either finds someone to sharpen them or else buys a new rock.

According to a story in *Sports Illustrated* written by J. A. Maxtone Graham several years ago, there appear to be only about four dozen practitioners of the art of making curling stones in the world, and most of them are employed in two factories in Scotland—one in Glasgow and the other just outside that city. Graham wrote that at Andrew Kay's, Mauchline, Ayrshire, the traditional methods for making curling stones are still used, and there you can see craftsmen with chisels chipping away at the dark-brown rock, called trevor, which comes from Wales. The Scottish Curling Stone Company in Glasgow uses more modern methods, mostly because it has sole access to the stone of Ailsa Craig, which is considered the best stone for

23

curling purposes in the world. (Ailsa stone, according to experts, is an aplitic alkaline igneous pluton composed of feldspar, quartz and pleochroic soda amphibole-riebeckite of pockolitic texture.)

As Graham wrote, Ailsa Craig is a huge, misshapen mass of granite rising up out of the sea 9 miles off the Robert Burns county of Ayrshire. The best Ailsa stone is either blue or red hone, each possessing a fine, close grain resistant to water and, therefore, frost (which, of course, can cause a stone to split). The Craig juts up in great vertical interlocking hexagonal pillars and the stone is blasted out with carefully placed charges of black powder, the object being to bring down one pillar at a time. After a pillar comes down, the surface of one section is drilled with little holes and a steel wedge put into each. A workman taps each wedge with a small hammer, and suddenly the mass gives a gentle shudder and opens up. Out of each hundred tons quarried, however, only one is usable in the manufacture of curling stones.

The process is expensive: when the rocks are shipped to the Scottish Curling Stone Company factory on the mainland they already cost almost $50 a pair, and by the time they have been shaped, polished and shipped across the Atlantic, the price may be anywhere between $80 to $200 for a pair. At this factory there are no men at work with chisels. Diamond-tipped cutting heads shape each Ailsa stone hunk into a solid cylinder; more diamonds chop the cylinder into curling-stone thicknesses called cheeses. About $12 worth of diamonds are used for each pair of stones. Then great lathes grasp the rough stones, and tungsten-carbide knives pare and shape them. The proper shape varies according to local demand. The running surface of the stone is slightly cupped, and what actually touches the ice is the tiny area of the circumference of the cup. The wider the cup, there-fore, the greater the touching area and the greater the friction.

Next comes polishing—the only truly manual process, Graham discovered. The stones are spun around on something like a potter's wheel, while skilled operators apply increasingly fine degrees of abrasive. After all this, some of the polish must be removed to make a 1½-inch-wide striking band around the circumference, for if two stones collided, polish to polish, the surface would be scarred. Traditionally, a man spent an hour with a rough-faced hammer forming the striking band, but now the area is blasted with steel shot.

These modern methods permit the making of stones guaranteed to weigh within 2 ounces, plus or minus, of the standard 40 pounds. What scares the curling world, though, is the fact that the supply of blue and red hone from Ailsa Craig probably will last only another century, and finding a durable substitute may be impossible. Given constant play on a rink, the surface of trevor may be expected to last for about 5 years while common Ailsa Craig will last from 7 to 8 years. The best hones generally last for about 12 years.

KEEPING SCORE

To the uninitiated, a curling scoreboard may look even more complicated than a baseball scorecard, but it is, in fact, quite simple to read and understand.

The middle line gives the score. The numbers in the lines above and below the score line show the ends that have been played and the team that won them. The scorekeeper simply places the number of the end above or below the number of points won in that end. Scoring is done on a cumulative basis, so, for instance, if, say, the White Rink has "1" under the 3 and "2" under the 5, it means that the Whites scored 3 points in the first end and then 2 points in the second end for a total of 5 points after two ends.

Let's look at the score of the hypothetical game shown in Diagram 3, below. Inspecting the board, the spectator can immediately see that the Whites defeated the Blacks 9 to 6 in a ten-end game. Here is an instant replay of what actually happened:

BLACK		4			6	9													
	1	2	3	4	5	6	7	8	9	10	11	12	13	14	15	16	17	18	BLANK ENDS
WHITE	1		2	3		5	7		10										8

Diagram 3

1st End: the Whites scored 1 point, so a "1" was placed on their line under the *1* on the middle line.

2nd End: the Whites scored 2 points, giving them a cumulative total of 3 points so far in the game, so the scorer placed a "2" under the 3 on the middle line. After two ends the Whites led 3 to 0.

3rd End: the Whites picked up another point; they now had 4 points. Note the number "3" under the 4.

4th End: the Blacks finally scored 2 points, and a "4" was placed above the 2 on the scoreboard.

5th End: the Whites, though, came back to score 2 more points, giving them a total of 6 points and—as you can see—a 6-to-2 lead over the Blacks halfway through the game.

6th End: the Blacks scored 3 points, giving them a total of 5 thus far, so the scorer then placed a "6" above the 5 on the middle line.

7th End: the Whites scored another point, giving them 7 points.

8th End: the Whites blanked this end, so neither team scored a point and an "8" was placed under the *Blank Ends* marker at the end of the scoreboard to denote that it was the White team that blanked the end.

9th End: the Blacks scored another point, giving them 6 points, with only one end left to play. So the Whites led 7 to 6.

10th End: the Whites scored 2 more points and finished with a total of 9 points, as the "10" below the 9 shows. Also note the "9" on the Blacks' line above the 6. So the final score was 9 to 6, the Whites winning.

3
The Delivery

CURLING, like golf, is a game of precision. In golf, for instance, the player tries to hit the ball as close to the hole as possible. In curling, the player tries to curl his stone as close to the button or the skip's designated target as possible. Curling, then, is a target game. Precision is the end result of constant practice. Practice, of course, develops a synchronized rhythm. And this rhythm, honed by hours and hours of practice, will produce a sound delivery that can be repeated under the stress and strain of competition. Such as playing in a bonspiel. You cannot possibly expect to come within striking distance of the skip's target if you don't have a dependable and fundamentally sound delivery. The best curlers have the best delivery. And a delivery hardly is a matter of luck.

The curler's delivery combines most of the elements of a golfer's swing and a baseball pitcher's windup. Like the golfer, the curler must have a sound grip, a solid stance, a firm takeaway, a consistent move forward, a perfectly timed release and a full-extension followthrough. Not to mention such things as proper weight shift, perfect balance and total concentration. And like the baseball pitcher, the curler must be able to release the rock with varying degrees of force and also must be able to control its direction.

Ernie has blended style and technique into what curlers the world over call a perfect marriage. Technically, his delivery is completely sound, totally flawless—right from the grip to the followthrough. Indeed, not only is Richardson the Sandy Koufax of curling, but also the Jack Nicklaus of curling.

In the old days there were dozens of curling deliveries, most of which were a terrible blend of style and technique—and there was little of either. Nevertheless, as bad as they were, these deliveries did get the job done to a certain extent. Two of the more popular old-style deliveries were the *push* and the *stationary swing*, and, in fact, many curlers still use these deliveries today. With the push delivery, the curler uses practically no backswing but simply pushes the rock down the ice with a forceful shove as he approaches the hog line. As you might imagine, this highly physical motion produces inconsistency since it lacks the necessary rhythm. With the stationary swing, the curler uses a shortened swing and little or no slide. This is not only another very inconsistent delivery; it also puts a heavy strain on the curler's back.

The best delivery—the one used by the great majority of the world's top curlers—might be called the *swing-slide delivery*. It definitely does not have a stationary swing or a push. Instead, it is a fluid, balanced movement that gets the job done with a minimum of physical effort and, depending upon how frequently the individual curler practices his game, a maximum of skill. The swing provides the momentum for the delivery, and the resultant motion provides the speed for the slide toward the hog line. This one-piece delivery depends upon perfect synchronization of the component parts.

However, before the curler grips his rock and steps into the hack to begin his delivery, he must put mind over matter. Skill in curling means nothing unless the player also has the qualities of intense concentration and supreme confidence. These two things are the trademarks of the best curlers.

28

1. *Concentration.* When you are involved in a curling game, you cannot be thinking about a problem at the office or tomorrow's schedule. You must dedicate yourself to the game at hand from the minute you step onto the ice until the minute you step off it. Daydreamers invariably lose their games. You must completely understand the shot that the skip wants you to play and concentrate solely on what you must do to make that shot. If he wants you to draw the rock, then don't be thinking about the take-out shot you played a few minutes before. If you do not completely understand the shot that the skip has signaled, ask him to call it for you again. Finally, try to imagine that you are the only person on the ice—that you are playing curling solitaire, so to speak. Concentrate on the shot you must make and forget the neighboring distractions. Even if the roof collapses, you should not be distracted. When the other players in the game are curling and you are standing off to the side, keep your mind on the situation and study what the ice does to the rocks as they pass down the sheet. If there is a bad spot on the ice, you should know it. And you do not pick up such important information by rushing into the lounge while the other players are curling. Indeed, curling demands absolute concentration through an entire game.

2. *Confidence.* Curlers must have confidence not only in their own ability to execute the shot that the skip has called, but also in the skip's ability to call the right shot. Confidence, which must not be confused with cockiness or conceit, is acquired only after hours and hours of practice—private practice, curling solitaire. This is where you work to perfect the fundamental techniques of your delivery and then repeatedly attempt to make the various shots that you always encounter in a competition. And also team practice, where you work with the skip and develop confidence that he always will call for the right shot.

Any time a curler has the slightest bit of self-doubt lingering in his mind as he prepares to make his shot, he most likely will miss the shot. Also, the best curlers never find themselves confronted with the so-called impossible shot. While they may not convert the impossible shot, the thought of failure never enters their minds during the periods of concentration and delivery. One other thing about confidence: It works in reverse. The more confidence you have in your game and the more good shots you make as a result, the less confidence your opponents will have.

Now you are ready to curl.

CLEANING THE STONE

Surely a scientist or an engineer one day must have said, "A moving object is subject to unexpected detours if foreign substances are on its surface." Consider the situation in other sports. Golfers constantly wash and wipe their golf balls to remove miniscule blotches of grass and smudges of dirt that can conspire to alter the direction of a ball in motion and reroute it away from its intended target. Baseball players always insist that the pitchers throw freshly scrubbed baseballs to them because smudgy, blotchy balls have a habit of performing tricks during their flight from the pitcher to the catcher and prove incredibly difficult to hit. And tennis players, of course, call for new tennis balls every few games to replace the grass-stained balls they had been using.

In curling, the situation is much the same, except that curlers do not call for new rocks every few ends or drop their dirty ones into a rock-washing machine. The curler himself must always make certain that the bottom of his rock is absolutely clean, completely free of loose impediments. Stones tend to pick up two particular types of foreign matter: (a) loose straw from the brooms and (b) shavings from the ice surface. Dirt of any sort on the bottom of the stone sends it off its intended course, and a dirty stone tends to pick up even more foreign matter on its way down the ice. The smallest piece of foreign substance on the bottom rim of the rock will raise the rim just enough to permit other pieces of dirt to slip under the stone and alter the speed and direction of the shot. A clean stone, on the other hand, tends to glide smoothly at the intended speed and in the intended direction, pushing aside the debris it encounters along the way.

30

Sweeping the bottom of the rock before delivery.

There is a "correct" way to clean your stone. First of all, set yourself in the hack with the rock placed on the ice a good distance away from you, between your left foot and the side of the sheet. (Left-handed curlers, of course, do the opposite.) Why here? Because it is one place that is not involved in any part of the delivery or the shot. In other words, never clean your rock in front of the hack. Now, simply turn the rock onto its side at about a 45-degree angle. You can set your left foot against the handle if you use both hands to clean the rock. Take the broom and sweep away all the loose impediments on the rim of the rock. Once you think you have finished, re-examine the surface of the rock to make certain that it is perfectly free of foreign matter. When done, sweep the debris off the ice in front of you.

31

Sweeping the ice in front of the hack before delivery.

As a final check, take the rock and slide it back and forth along the ice. If it slides easily, without any apparent roughness, it is clean. If it rides bumpily, brush the bottom surface again. Remember: you cannot expect to make even the easiest curling shot if your rock has dirt on it.

CLEANING THE SLIDING FOOT

Too many curlers forget this important job. The sliding foot (the left foot for right-handed curlers, the right foot for left-handed curlers) must also be free from loose straw and ice shavings or else it, too, will tend to stray from its intended route during the delivery. Before getting into the hack, scrape your sliding foot on the backboards behind the hack. Then inspect the sole carefully to be sure it's clean. Or, once in the hack, simply take the broom and place it under the sliding foot and sweep away all the loose impediments that have found a home on the bottom of the shoe or boot. Sometimes ice shavings will mat on the bottom, and have to be scraped away with the broom. But whatever effort it takes, always have a clean sliding foot.

WARM-UPS

There is really no such thing as a warm-up in curling. As a result, many curlers usually miss their first few shots in a game because they have not had a chance to let their body get accustomed to the motion of delivering the rock. To prevent this type of bad start, Richardson thinks that all curlers should go through a short series of exercises on the ice to get themselves loose. He suggests:

"Do some bends from the waist and then a few knee bends and knee springs. Nothing too extreme, mind you, but enough to get unwound. And also exercise your arms, extending them in various directions to loosen the muscles. Doing these exercises on the ice and not in the lounge or the locker room is very important. After all, the temperature in the rink is always considerably lower than the temperature in the heated lounge and locker room. I've found—and so will you—that pregame exercises invariably prevent early-game blues."

THE STANCE IN THE HACK

Like all sports, curling places a premium on the correct start. In fact, without a proper start, a curler has little hope of successfully completing his shot. Once again, you can compare the curler's so-called "position at address" with the stance of the golfer. He, too, must address the ball correctly, with feet, hands, shoulders, head and body weight all in proper position or else he definitely will mis-hit his shot.

The first rule for a good stance is to be comfortable and relaxed. You cannot be too tight when you are in the hack. If

33

your muscles are tight and fighting one another, the result will be a herky-jerky delivery that hardly will produce a good shot. Stay relaxed, though not so much so that your concentration wavers. All curlers seem to have some little idiosyncrasy that relaxes them. Some may tug at their trousers, others may crane their neck and still others may simply take a long, deep breath. Some curlers like to wiggle while they are in the hack, too, just the way many golfers wiggle. In fact, the curler, like the golfer, should try to remain in motion for as long as possible as he remains in the hack. Only when he is ready to start his delivery should he become absolutely motionless. Again, this is a highly individualized matter, and each curler has his own way of getting comfortable in the hack. That's perfectly all right. The big thing is to be comfortable, regardless of how you do it.

A comfortable position also creates the feel for the shot you have to make. You should have a sense of total confidence in your ability to make the shot that the skip has called for. If you do not have that confidence, you are not comfortable.

Positioning the Feet in the Hack

First of all, a brief reminder. Ice shavings oftentimes accumulate in the hack and freeze against the hard rubber, and as a result many curlers skid uncontrollably when they move away from the hack, ruining their entire delivery right at the start. This is a particular problem for left-handed curlers, since they are outnumbered by about 10 to 1 and their hack is used much less than the right-handed curler's hack. To eliminate the possibility of a skidding start, curlers should place a glove in the hack underneath their shoe or boot. This will help ensure a solid, skidless start.

The right foot is the pivot for the entire shot in curling. Unless it is set correctly, not only position-wise but also weight-wise, you cannot expect to make a good shot. To take the correct stance, start off by getting down in a squatting position. Now put your right foot in the hack so that the ball of your right foot rests squarely against the back of the hack. The toe of your right shoe

Position in the hack at the address, as viewed from the right. Note that the right arm is extended but not rigid or tensed.

Position in the hack, as viewed from the left. Note the angle of the broom.

Front view of the position in the hack. Note that the knees are
parallel to the center line.

or boot should be pointed straight ahead, not to either side. After all, the position of your right foot in the hack sets the direction of your body—and if your toe is not aligned correctly, then your body will be off line, too, and a misdirected shot will certainly be the result. You can double-check the direction of your right toe by making certain it is absolutely parallel to the center line.

The position of the left foot depends on the crouching position, and is a matter of individual preference. "My left foot," Richardson says, "is just slightly ahead of the right by only a few inches." He squats in a very upright pose, and his left foot remains almost alongside the right one so that he can maintain good balance in the hack. Curlers who hunch forward in the hack place their left foot well ahead of their right foot. The left foot provides the balance. Just find the most comfortable, stable and balanced position for your particular stance and stick with it.

Positioning the Knees

This, like positioning the toe of the right foot in the hack, is a delicate matter. Both knees should be perfectly parallel to the center line (see photo on page 37). When they are out of position, the hips and the shoulders tend to turn away in the wrong direction during the delivery, and a variety of bad shots can result. Also, don't let your knees touch the ice during your stance or your delivery. If they accidentally do so, they will upset the delicate balance you have worked so hard to attain.

Positioning the Hips and Shoulders

Both the hips and the shoulders should be set absolutely straight forward and at perfect right angles to the delivery or center line. This ensures that two imaginary lines drawn across the hips and across the shoulders would be parallel to the ice surface. If the shoulders or the hips are tilted too much in any direction, a mis-hit shot almost certainly will be the result. Since the right arm (of right-handed curlers) grips the rock, the right shoulder becomes the so-called "hinge" during the delivery. Consequently, it is imperative that you not allow your right shoulder to stray away from that position. If you drop your right shoulder too much during the delivery, the stone will come into contact with the ice well in advance of the intended spot. If you raise your shoulder, you will over-shoot the planned contact position and land your rock too far forward.

Positioning the Head

If the hips and the shoulders are in proper position, then the back will be perfectly straight. All this helps make the positioning of the head a relatively simple matter. Your head should be erect, with your chin up, so that your eyes can be fixed squarely on the target—the skip's broom—at the other end of the ice. Keep them there throughout the delivery. When you move your eyes off the target, you invariably miss the shot.

Positioning the Arms and the Rock

The position of the rock dictates the position of both arms during the delivery. At the address position in the hack you should slide the stone forward as far as possible with your right arm without pulling your shoulders, hips, knees, legs or head out of position. This becomes the correct position for your right arm. It is important not to let your right arm be rigid or tense; it should be extended forward comfortably, without any muscular stress. The set position for the stone depends upon the feel you have for the shot that the skip has called. While some people think the rock should be centered on the center line, this is not really the correct approach. The position of the stone is an individual thing, mostly dependent upon a curler's particular curling style. Whatever its position, the rock should be almost an extension of the relaxed arm. Whatever you do, don't play muscleman with your arms. Muscular, taut extensions produce jerky motions that have no place in a smooth delivery.

The proper position for the left arm at address also depends upon the individual curler. The left arm and the broom serve as a counterbalance for the right arm. The natural tendency in curling would be for the curler's entire right side—the side on which he picks up the 40-pound rock—to collapse somewhat during the delivery. But the left arm neutralizes this problem

Position of the left arm and broom as Richardson slides the rock slightly forward preparatory to going into the backswing.

of maintaining balance. (See photo on page 36.) More than 99 per cent of curlers keep their broom in their left hand to aid their balance during the delivery. But, as Richardson attests, it's not a very easy thing to control. He tucks the broom handle under his left arm, almost sticking it into his armpit, and then points the broom itself at about a 45-degree angle to his left. Like the right arm, the left arm must be extended in a comfortable position, not taut, not tense. "You'll know when you feel comfortable," Richardson says. "Or better yet, you'll know when you're uncomfortable. Balance is something you can feel, so work at it."

Distributing Body Weight in the Hack

Golfers are taught to keep their body weight evenly distributed between both feet during the address position. Well, the same rule applies to curling. As you assume your position in the hack, with arms properly extended and the rock resting on the ice surface, your weight also should be distributed evenly on your right and left feet. Any imbalance will create a problem that eventually will force you to make at least one other mistake somewhere during delivery. Two or more wrongs never make a right.

THE GRIP

It goes almost without saying that curlers must have strong fingers. The rock, after all, weighs 40 pounds, and you do grip the handle of it with your fingers. Golfers are told to grip their clubs much the way they hold a pencil: delicately. Curlers are told the same thing, even though it does sound somewhat absurd to tell someone that he should hold a 40-pound rock "delicately." Let Ernie Richardson explain: "What we mean by 'delicate' in curling is simply an exaggeration of 'feeling.' In other words, we don't want curlers to clutch the handle of the rock in their fist; instead, we want them to caress it, to hold it with definite feeling."

The most common fault of beginning curlers is that they do

not hold the rock properly—delicately, with the fingers. Only if you do so can you then make the natural, flowing swing backward and then forward that a good delivery demands. If you grasp the handle in your fist and try to strangle it, you will not have a smooth swing and in the end you will have to push the rock down ice with a violent thrust. Here is how you should grip the rock:

Wrap the tips of your fingers underneath the handle. The index, third and fourth fingers should all be on the ivory part of the handle; the little finger should be at the very end, barely touching the ivory. The handle of the rock should rest across the fingers on a line from the first joint of the little finger to the second joint of the index finger. The thumb overlaps the top of the handle slightly and rests on the neck of the handle—actually right on the shaft. As you look at the grip, you should notice the formation of a V between the thumb and the index finger.

The fingers all play different roles during the delivery. The thumb gives you the feel of the rock while you take your backswing, and along with the little finger it permits you to apply the particular turn you want for the shot. The index finger provides most of the pressure throughout the delivery, with help from the middle finger. The fourth finger goes along mostly for the ride, although it also may be used to steady the handle. The little finger applies practically no pressure but helps guide the rock during delivery.

Curlers with small hands should make slight modifications in the finger action: Use all four fingers of your hand as pressure points because your index and middle fingers will not provide enough pressure for the shot. Fingertip control provides the force you need for the shot you are trying to make, and it produces the smooth, swinging delivery you want—not a push. It is also the only way you can gauge the shot you have to make.

The Out-Turn Grip

According to Richardson, when you grip the rock for the out-turn, which produces a left-to-right action, "Either keep the

The out-turn. Note that the handle of the stone is turned to about one o'clock in the first picture, and the hand is pointed along the intended line of delivery after the rock has been released.

handle of the rock straight down the line of delivery, or turn it clockwise to about one o'clock." He himself prefers to turn the handle because, as he says, "When my hand straightens on the downswing, a gentle turn automatically results and provides a free and easy delivery."

The out-turn (continued)

Richardson offers a word of caution, however: "An exaggerated turn will produce a 'spinner,' a shot that is well off the target at the other end of the ice. Your stone should make only about three or four turns from the time it leaves your hand until it reaches the target. If you exaggerate the turn initially, the stone will make five or more turns and probably miss the broom."

The out-turn (continued)

When you set yourself for the out-turn delivery, make certain there is no tightening of your fingers or your muscles. Your hand should rest comfortably on the handle as you move it into the clockwise position. Otherwise you will not have a free and easy pendulum movement during the delivery.

The out-turn (continued)

The In-Turn Grip

This grip produces a right-to-left action. For the in-turn grip, Richardson says, "The handle should be either straight on the delivery line or turned counterclockwise to about eleven o'clock." He prefers to turn the handle because it best suits his particular curling style. Either way—straight or turned counterclockwise—is correct. As in the out-turn grip, your fingers and muscles must not tighten up.

The in-turn. Note that the handle is turned to about the eleven o'clock position in the first photo.

The in-turn (continued)

The in-turn (continued)

The in-turn (continued)

Turn and Spin

All curlers must study the results of their out-turn and in-turn deliveries to determine the peculiarities of turn and spin that apply particularly to them. No two curlers impart the same amount of spin to the same shot. And all curlers impart more spin or turn to one type of shot than they do to the other. Curlers have been known to make their out-turn shots spin four times during the slide down the ice and their in-turn shots spin only twice during the trip. The more a stone spins, the farther it travels and the less it curls. Normally, a rock that spins between two and four times produces the best results. A stone that spins less than two full turns is not good either because it could lose its turn by the time it reaches its target. By knowing the particular limitations of his deliveries, a curler should be able to compensate for them by using more or less ice or more or less weight with his shot. You acquire this knowledge through lots of private practice.

THE BACKSWING

"Every curler is suited to a different style of delivery," says Ernie Richardson. "I've seen short men who lift the rock extremely high—almost above the shoulder—on the backswing, and I've seen tall men with practically no backswing. Nothing about the backswing surprises me any more." Richardson, who stands 6 feet 4 inches, has a very short backswing. His brother Sam, who is a few inches shorter, has a very high, 3-foot backswing. Then there is Bob Pickering, who for years has been one of the top curlers in Canada. Although he is short, Pickering has an unusually high, arcing backswing. "I wouldn't suggest that any curlers copy Bob, although he is a fine player," Richardson says. "Bob is so successful because he somehow manages to bring the rock down very gently onto the ice. He told me he uses that style because years ago he found it was the best way to compensate for the thaw and the water that used to settle on

The backswing. The left foot moves backward and to the side

the ice. While ice conditions have improved greatly over the years, Bob still uses the high backswing—and, considering his record, he uses it well."

The backswing is easily the most important part of the entire delivery. If the curler does not take the rock back along the line of his intended delivery and then bring it forward squarely on the same line, he of course will miss his shot. The backswing,

as the right arm moves back.

then, must almost be an extension of the curler's delivery line. Imagine a straight line always drawn between the rock in the backswing and the skip's broom, or target, at the opposite end of the ice. The rock must always remain consistent with the line of direction.

There are two important things to remember as you start your backswing: Your body must be set squarely at the target, and

A front view of the top of the backswing. Richardson's eyes are fixed on the skip's broom at the other end of the ice.

your eyes must be fixed on the skip's broom. Some curlers make the mistake of looking at the rock they are supposed to hit instead of the skip's broom. This is a tragic error, for it causes the curler to throw his stone inside the broom every time. *Play for the skip's broom—not the rock he wants you to hit.*

The mechanics of the backswing are fairly natural. Most of your body weight should rest on your right foot as you are crouched in the hack ready to begin your motion backward. Take the stone back with your fingers—*delicately*, remember—and then straighten out your right knee. At the same time, move your left foot back and somewhat sideward, almost in perfect harmony with the movement of your right arm. As this happens, your body will naturally begin to rise. It is very important that your hips, shoulders and head all remain square on the target and that your eyes remain fixed on the skip's broom. Meanwhile, the stone itself seems almost suspended from the fingers of your right hand, with the right shoulder acting as the fulcrum during the swing. Golf has much the same action during the backswing.

The length of the backswing is a matter of individual preference. Although Richardson brings the rock back only 5 or 6 inches off the ice at the most, there are curlers who bring it back 3 feet and even higher. One question new curlers always ask their teachers is: "Is there a forward press in curling?" A forward press, of course, is the starting point for any movement backward, the point at which all other motion stops and the backward motion begins. Golfers, for instance, tend to press their hands forward just an inch or two the second before they take the club back. This is their forward press. In curling, though, there is no need for such a movement. You should be comfortable as you start your backswing, and any motion beforehand will only tend to make you uncomfortable. Once you feel set in the hack, begin the backswing. Don't make any excess movements because more often than not they will disrupt the tempo and the feeling that you already have established for the shot.

During the backswing, the relative position of the broom in your left hand also is a matter of individual preference. The broom, remember, acts as a counterbalance throughout the delivery. Simply keep the broom away from your body in a position that enables you to maintain perfect balance throughout the backswing.

55

THE DOWNSWING

The downswing begins, naturally enough, at the top of the backswing and is, for all practical purposes, the backswing in reverse. The trick is to return to your starting position without losing any of the balance, concentration and confidence you had when you began your backswing. In Richardson's words, "Curling would be easier without the backswing and the downswing —but then it wouldn't be the same game!"

The downswing. The left foot comes forward as he swings the

rock forward in a smooth, pendulumlike motion.

A front view of the downswing. The broom helps Richardson to maintain balance. His right arm leads his body; his weight has shifted to his left foot.

At the top of the backswing, as you are ready to start the downswing, there is what golfers call "the pause at the top"—that fleeting moment between the end of the backward motion and the beginning of the forward motion. As you pause momentarily, your body should still be in perfect balance. Your right arm has reached the top of its pendulum; it has no place to go but down. At that instant of the pause the stone seems to dangle from your fingers. Then, suddenly, the weight of the stone starts the right arm swinging forward along the same trajectory on which it just passed. Whatever you do, don't force your downswing or you will ruin your chances for making the shot your skip wants.

As you start down, body weight becomes terribly important. Many curlers lose their balance during their downswing as a result of an improper transfer of body weight, and then they have little chance for making a solid shot. Set back in the hack, with almost all of your body weight resting on your right foot and the stone at the top of its pendulum, you begin the downswing by moving your right arm forward. Your right knee begins to bend at the same time your left foot starts forward—and so does your left arm, which is holding the broom. The broom, of course, is still helping your balance. Your right arm and left foot should move forward at almost the same speed. This balanced combination of moving right arm and moving left foot will enable you to keep your head, shoulders and hips in their proper squared position, directly on the target.

Like golfers, curlers must have a very rhythmical downswing, free of any exaggerated or stiff motions. Let the stone do the work for you—don't force it. Remember to maintain a firm, but not tense, right arm throughout the downswing. If your elbow is bent too much, you will misplay your shot because you will have to make some type of unnatural, exaggerated motion at delivery. The best way to make certain that you maintain the correct arm position during the downswing is to swing the rock completely down, out and through in a smooth pendulumlike motion. Don't jerk the stone at any point.

As you practice your downswing, with the rock properly extended, you must take great pains to "stay behind the rock." What does that mean? Richardson says, "Beginning curlers and, for that matter, even the most experienced curlers tend to let their body lead the rock during the downswing. They let their arm drag behind their shoulders and legs. The arm must lead —or else." A proper downswing, with the shoulders and legs following the arm, enables the curler to sight the target with his rock as it moves ahead of him into the proper delivery motion. But when the arm trails the shoulders and legs, he loses much of the feel for the shot he must make, and he never really sights the rock until it has left his hand.

One more thing: There is a correct time during the downswing when you must apply the particular turn—either the in-turn or the out-turn—that you want for the shot you are making. That correct time, though, depends upon the individual curler. However, don't make the mistake of waiting until you set the rock onto the ice before you apply the turn to the handle. There's no way that will work. Start applying it gradually as you move your arm forward. Find a spot in your downswing where you can comfortably begin to apply the turn—and stick with it. Remember that the handle should already be turning as you let go of your stone.

While moving through the downswing, Richardson advises you to concentrate your efforts totally on acquiring a smooth, fluid contact with the ice while keeping your body straight and your eyes fixed on the skip's broom at the other end of the ice. "It all takes hours and hours of practice," he says. "It is a matter of finesse acquired by hours in the rink."

As the stone touches down, the right leg straightens out, the left knee bends more to lower the body further and your weight transfers to the left foot. A word of caution: You must make certain that the stone makes contact with the ice in a position slightly ahead of the left foot. If the stone lags behind the left foot on impact, the pendulum swing has been obviously disturbed. During the actual delivery itself, your left foot should be almost directly behind the rock—and, of course, almost all your body weight remains on that left foot as you slide forward with your followthrough.

A final reminder: Practice long and hard to develop a fluid downswing, with your right arm leading and your body weight smoothly shifting from right foot to left. Think of it this way: How can you expect to make the shot the skip has called if you don't keep yourself and your rock in the correct release position?

THE SLIDE AND FOLLOWTHROUGH

After a stone is released, the curler should continue to slide forward, his eye still on the broom, his right arm and hand still extended and pointed along the line of delivery. The slide is the natural followthrough to a good delivery and it demands a great deal of practice to execute it properly.

The most important aspect of the slide involves the sliding foot—the left foot for right-handed curlers, the right foot for left-handed players. Slides vary in length; the length depends upon the manner in which the curler exercises control with his sliding foot—meaning that it can also be used as a brake. The sole of the shoe or boot on the sliding foot should be hard and slick. "Never use new shoes or boots in a curling competition," Richardson advises. "Make certain that the soles are old enough to have plenty of slide." As mentioned earlier, a separate slider can be worn. No matter what you wear, the sole of the sliding foot must be kept completely clean of ice shavings and straw.

It is up to the curler to decide how long his slide should be. "My slide takes me only about 15 or 16 feet from the hack—that's about halfway to the hog line. I know some curlers who slide right to the edge of the hog line and some who don't slide even 5 feet."

One word of warning, especially to young players: many curlers slide too far and then have to fight it in order to avoid going over the hog line. If a curler does so, his rock should be removed from play. Also, if you have an unusually long slide, you are obviously aware throughout delivery that you will have to fight your forward movement at some point. This makes it hard to control the various weights you must apply to your rock—it's not easy to be concentrating on the shot your skip has called for if you're worried about crossing that hog line. It puts undue pressure on you during delivery.

However, don't start trying to shorten, or lengthen, your slide to the extent that your balance and control are affected. Off-

On this page and the following two, Richardson demonstrates what happens when too much weight is put on the broom during the slide. His body is twisted and turned off the intended line of delivery—and the stone has little chance of reaching its target.

balance slides produce poor shots that not only don't have the correct weight but also almost never find the skip's target.

Like many curlers, Ernie Richardson uses his broom to help maintain his balance during the slide. "However," he points out, "I don't put too much weight on it when it touches down onto the ice. On the other hand, there are a lot of curlers who hold the broom straight out in the air and do *not* use it for balancing purposes. Instead they use their left foot—the sliding foot—

to maintain balance throughout the slide. In fact, the curlers who basically ignore the broom for balancing and depend strictly on their left foot have perhaps the nicest form of delivery you will ever see. When the broom is straight out and you are balanced like a tightrope walker at 250 feet, it is indeed a beautiful sight. But not many curlers can do it because it takes constant practice. My cousin, Arnold Richardson, who was the vice-skip on our championship teams, perfected this style, and most people think he still has the smoothest delivery in curling."

A final word of warning on the use of the broom: If you decide to use your broom for balance in the delivery, don't put too much body weight on it. If you do, you will twist your body around and pull yourself off the intended line of delivery. As a result, you'll have little chance of making your shot. Remember that it is more difficult to control your balance with your broom than with your sliding foot.

During the slide, keep your right arm fully extended forward even though your fingers have released the rock. There should almost be a straight line along the delivery line from the sliding rock to your right arm to your right eye and back to your trailing right foot. Don't force your right arm out at the sliding rock, though, because that will mean you have forced the shot itself. How far you slide down the ice toward the hog line depends, of course, upon the thrust behind the push-off you make with your right foot and leg from the hack as well as on the way you use your sliding foot. Richardson's advice: "Let your slide be very natural—and don't let it influence anything in the delivery that precedes it. A good, sound slide preceded by a bad backswing and downswing will only result in a missed shot."

Richardson also offers several points for you to check if you are having problems with your followthrough: "I find myself lapsing into these very basic mistakes, and I suspect there may be many other curlers who also find themselves making poor slides that ruin their shots." Here is his checklist of Don'ts:

1. *Don't* push the rock down the ice. Let it start away gently, settling onto the ice in the same level way that an airplane lands on a runway. If you do end up pushing the rock down ice, it means that your delivery was bad somewhere in the backswing or the downswing.

2. *Don't* use any exaggerated hand motions as you let go of the handle of the rock. Curlers who insist upon a flourishing withdrawal of their right hand risk hitting the moving handle with their hand and sending the rock completely off course. Once you release the rock, let your hand and arm continue to point along the same line of delivery as the rock itself. If you do this consistently, you will have a better delivery.

65

The slide. Note that the right arm is kept fully extended until he stops his slide.

3. Once you release the rock, *don't* alter your body position until you come to a complete stop. Many curlers like to jump up or move their heads or bend their arms once they have released the rock. These actions destroy the natural follow-through that is so important to making a good shot. Also, if you stay in the same position and keep your eye on the skip's broom, you will be able to judge whether the shot is good or bad before the stone reaches the other end of the ice. You'll learn what went wrong and how to correct it.

4. *Don't* slide sideways down the ice; keep directly behind the rock.

5. *Don't* slide across the hog line.

PUTTING IT ALL TOGETHER

The following sequence of photographs show Ernie Richardson's delivery from position in the hack to the stand-up at the end of the followthrough.

The complete delivery, from the address to the stand-up at the end of the followthrough. Note that Richardson continues to watch the rock as it travels down the ice, in order to see if it reaches its target.

7

8

11

12

13

14

15

16

4
Weight: What It Means

IN curling, "weight" is the amount of force, or momentum, on the stone as it moves down the ice. The curler must, of course, apply the weight for each shot he makes, depending upon the call made by his skip. Some curlers use their backswing as a means of supplying weight to the shot. For instance, they may take a long, high backswing for a speed shot—that is, a shot the skip wants played through the house or one that will take out one or more opposition rocks. Or they may take a shorter, lower backswing for a draw shot, since it, unlike, say, the speed shot, demands finesse. All in all, Ernie Richardson thinks this is a good technique for the beginning curler. "By using a backswing with various levels," he explains, "the curler avoids the problem of eventually having to push the rock down the ice. This method also enables him to have the weight of the shot well under control before he begins the forward swing that leads to the release of the rock itself."

He dislikes the "push" method of applying weight to a shot because "most curlers are not strong enough to play that way.

There are a few exceptions, of course. The one whose name immediately comes to mind is Hec Gervais of Edmonton, Alberta. He has won many bonspiel championships with his very effective 'pushing' style. But Hec weighs about 260 pounds, give or take a few, and at the end of his delivery he is strong enough to flick the rock the way most of us flip a pebble."

Nevertheless, Richardson does not use the backswing for controlling the weight of his shots. "I prefer to depend on my leg drive as a gauge for weight," he says. "I can do this because I've played the game for so long and I've practiced it for countless hours. But the average curler should use the backswing method."

There are various types of weight to apply to shots. For instance, there is *draw weight* when the skip wants the curler to play his rock into the house. *Guard weight* is applied when the skip wants the curler's rock to stop in front of the rings and block out either a teammate's rock or a rival's rock. A player applies *tap weight* when the skip wants him to curl around some short guards or barely nudge a rival rock out of position. And there is *straight hitting weight,* which a curler uses when the skip wants the rock thrown with enough speed and force to push an opposition rock through the house and out of play. "There's also the quiet take-out weight," Richardson adds. "That's when the player completely misses the shot his skip has called. It's an 'in' joke in curling."

Weight, like so many other things in curling, depends upon the individual curler's feel for a shot. It comes down to concentration again. You have the feel for a shot or you don't have it. It's that simple. When you sit in the hack, the only thing you should be thinking about is the shot and the weight that you are about to play. If your concentration wavers, forget it.

The condition of the ice is an important factor in deciding how much weight to apply. By observing how the first stones in a game travel down the ice and by watching for surface changes during the game, the skip and his rinkmates can adjust weight as needed. Concentration along with observation and analysis are needed throughout the game.

5
Sweeping

STATED simply, the sweepers on a team help to steer a rock down the ice toward its intended target. For one thing, they clear away any loose straw and chips of ice in front of the rock that might send it off course. But that isn't the only reason why sweeping is so important in curling. Air in motion exerts less pressure on an object than air at rest. Sweeping stirs up the air, of course, and as a result, the moving rock passes along with less pressure from the air. Vigorous sweeping also makes the ice smoother, therefore the stone meets less surface resistance. Sweeping is a very important part of curling. Good sweeping can affect the length of a throw by as much as 10 or 15 feet, in addition to helping maintain the direction of the moving stone.

Besides the obvious physical reasons for sweeping, there also are psychological ones. For instance, without sweeping, there would be only one curler in action at a time. The other curlers in the game would be mere spectators. It would be boring to just stand around and wait their turns. With sweeping, all the players feel, not only that they are involved, but that there is a special *need* for them—that, as the saying goes, "They couldn't win without me." And as the records prove, sweepers have turned many a poor shot into a great one. Says Richardson, "Good sweeping has saved me not only when I was playing my rock but also when I was the skip. Many times I gave a player the wrong broom for his shot but was saved from disaster by superior sweeping. And many times I have shot a little too light and my sweepers have worked the rock into the house."

Two sweepers can start sweeping as soon as the player has released the rock, and although the skip may call out instructions to them, they should have control of the rock for about three quarters of the way down the ice; then the skip's judgment takes over. He can leave the house and help sweep to bring the stone into the house. Anyone can sweep beyond the tee line, but *only one person at a time*. The rival skip can also sweep to try to make the stone go through the house and out of play.

Like many skips, Ernie Richardson is a so-called "holler guy." He watches the initial movement of the rock, and then the noise begins. "If the throw obviously is beyond my broom area, I yell, 'Whoa!' Then the sweepers stop sweeping—the slower the rock moves, of course, the more it will draw into the target. However, if the rock seems to be so light that it might not reach the target, I yell, 'Sweep! Sweep!' And they get right to work with their brooms so the stone will travel faster. Personally, I feel the skip should direct traffic on the ice as much as possible. I also feel that the players in the game always like to know exactly what is going on, so why not tell them? In ice hockey, the best goalies are the noisy ones—they keep their defensemen informed of the action around them. In curling, the best skips are the noisy ones."

THE GRIP

There are two basic grips for the broom, both fundamentally sound and both totally acceptable.

82

The over grip, showing the position of the left hand on the broom handle.

The Over Grip

Grip the top of the handle lightly, yet firmly, with the fingers of your right hand (left hand, of course, for left-handed curlers). Put your left hand as far down on the handle as you need in order to have good leverage. The palm of your hand should face your body, the thumb pointing downward. Make sure that your left hand grips the handle only with the fingers—never wrap the handle in your palm. Finger touch permits you to obtain maximum wrist movement and provides the flipping action so important for hard sweeping. The right hand applies pressure and serves as the hinge for the back-and-forth action.

The under grip, showing the position of the left hand on the broom handle.

The Under Grip

With this grip, the top—or right—hand is in the same position as the top hand in the over grip. However, the bottom hand is placed so that the palm faces away from the sweeper's body, thumb pointing up.

While Ernie Richardson prefers the over grip, he says, "Select the grip that feels most natural and most comfortable for you." Not using the same grip as one of the world's greatest curlers would hardly be a mistake.

SWEEPING TECHNIQUE

Sweeping looks considerably easier than it actually is, and many hours of practice are required to develop the correct technique. Beginners should start learning how to sweep properly by sweeping without moving their feet. As a basic rule, right-handed sweepers should sweep on the left side of the moving rock, and left-handed sweepers should sweep on the right side. Since there are more right-handed people, many times—but not always—both sweepers will be on the same side, one in front of the other.

1. Grip your broom, bend your knees and your back until your eyes are directly on an imaginary rock.

2. Spread your feet far enough apart for you to be able to maintain excellent balance on the ice.

3. Start sweeping back and forth in this "still" position. You will find that you'll be moving your feet in order to keep your balance. Whatever direction your feet happen to move is the proper way for you to maintain your balance—as simple as that may sound. Whatever you do, never cross your feet.

4. Start moving down the ice. Gradually increase sweeping speed.

5. Practice with a moving rock.

You must never touch your sweeping partner's broom. If you do, you undoubtedly will cause a "burned rock"—one that has been touched by a broom during the sweeping and therefore removed from play.

One more suggestion: While sweeping, try to keep glancing in the direction of the house, toward which the moving rock is headed. By doing so, you will be able to get a better idea of what is needed to make the shot.

While sweepers generally depend on the skip for instructions, they also should learn how to judge the condition of the ice surface and the weight of a moving stone and how to sweep for it. Also they need to know their teammates' abilities and be ready to help them make difficult shots. For instance, if the skip calls for a take-out shot and the player throws inside the skip's broom, the sweepers must sweep the ice very hard in order to keep the rock moving as fast as possible so that it won't curl as much and still may make the shot.

Sweepers should not exhaust themselves needlessly or too soon, and they should remain hovered over a moving rock until

Richardson demonstrates sweeping the ice in front of a moving rock.

it has passed the tee line—if, indeed, it does so. Countless shots have been missed because the sweepers quit too soon when perhaps a few more swishes of the broom might have made the difference between a successful shot and a bad one.

6
Strategy

FORMING A RINK

Putting together a winning team in any sport takes considerable time and a great deal of patience. Molding different personalities, different temperaments and different skills into a smooth-functioning unit is something that can hardly be done overnight. As Ernie Richardson says, "You can take the four best curlers in the world, put them together and yet have one of the worst rinks imaginable. The best curling rinks consist of a delicate blend of all the finer points of the game. For instance, you don't want a team composed of four players expert at draw shots but weak on take-outs. Finding four compatible curlers is not easy, believe me."

One of the best rinks ever put together was the famed Richardson Rink. Ernie Richardson was the skip. Ernie's cousin, Arnold, was the third or the vice-skip; his brother Garnet was the second; his cousin Wes was the lead. Starting in 1959, the Richardson Rink dominated the world of curling in much the same way the New York Yankees used to dominate baseball and the Boston

89

Celtics used to dominate basketball. The Richardsons won four MacDonald Briers (Canadian championships) in five years—an incredible accomplishment. They also won four Scotch Cups (international championships), five provincial championships, a Masters title and also a Tournament of Champions. And, Ernie Richardson adds, "There's no telling how many cash spiels we won during those years."

One year Wes Richardson, the lead, hurt his back, so Ernie recruited Mel Perry to replace him. "Mel fitted in perfectly," Ernie said. "We played more than one hundred games the year Mel was the lead, and we lost only seven. On top of that, we won every championship we entered."

Let Ernie describe how the Richardson Rink operated:

"We ate, slept and thought curling twenty-four hours a day. We decided to get serious about the game, so we sacrificed our free time and took off from work to play in as many bonspiels as we could. We really had the perfect team: four guys who thought alike. Garnet—we all call him Sam—was the holler guy on the team. When things were not going too well and we were down in a game, Sam would cheer us up with his comments. He was our spirit guy. He was also our best sweeper. Wes was a good sweeper too. Now Arnold was the quiet man. He never said anything. I don't think he even knows the meaning of the word 'argue.' He was the ideal third or vice-skip. Once we made the commitment to compete everywhere, we curled four and five hours a day. We'd practice at the rink on the way home from work and we curled many a morning when we weren't working. It all paid off."

The Lead

Basically, according to the Richardson formula, the makeup of a rink should follow a strategical design. The lead should be able to make draw shots with great consistency. He does not have to be a strong take-out player, but if he can play to the rings fairly well, this tactic keeps the opposition on the defensive. The lead should be a strong sweeper, so he needs to be in really good physical shape, because in curling competitions he might have to sweep four or five games in one day—a difficult assignment and one too demanding for anyone not in the best of condition.

The Second

The second must be a fine hitter, and also a strong sweeper. He should always be able to come up with a double if the lead happens to miss that shot; that is, he should be able to take out one rock and then roll over and take out the other. So the second must be able to play the finesse shots—unlike the lead.

One other important thing about the lead and the second: Both of them have to be satisfied with their positions on the team. The lead and the second must offer strong morale. Too many good rinks have been ruined because one or the other was not particularly happy with his role and figured he was better than, say, the skip. It is most important that they have total confidence in the skip. Otherwise the rink will hardly be a team in the true sense.

The Third, or Vice-Skip

The third must be able to play the fine shots. The vice-skip actually has to be able to play the same shots as the skip—only he does not throw last. Slow taps, raised shots, draw shots around guards, take-out shots—everything. As vice-skip, he also has to know the ice as well as the skip himself. While the third does not necessarily have to be a good sweeper, he needs to be able to judge the weight of incoming stones so that he can instruct the sweepers. Because he stands in the house and holds the broom for the skip, he should understand the strategy of the game.

The Skip

The skip has to be able to play every shot in the book, and also know when to call them. He must have great draw weight—that is, his draw shots have to be strong enough to go against two, three or four stones in order to save a point or an end for his team. He has to praise and encourage his players to keep their morale and confidence high, and he must have a good disposition and an even temper. "I learned very early in my curling career that the skip has to take the good with the bad," Richardson recalls. But the most important quality a skip must have is the ability to play under pressure, since games invariably depend on the talents of the skip playing the last rock. Richardson's advice: "If you cannot play under pressure, then become the lead or the second."

As the team strategist, the skip must decide where and how his team's rocks should be played. In addition he must be able to determine everything there is to know about the condition of the ice and the abilities not only of his teammates but also of the rival players, so that he can take advantage of the opposition's weaknesses. If, for example, the rival third cannot play out-turn hits with any degree of accuracy, the skip should set the house in such order that the rival third will be forced to play the out-turns. The other team's morale can be affected by such strategy, and it also increases your team's confidence in you as skip.

Incidentally, Richardson, one of the greatest skips in curling history, claims that he learned how to remain cool and confident under pressure by playing pool and poker. "Confidence is something you must acquire at an early age. I was not a cocky kid, but I was confident. I always felt as though I would win at pool and, later, at poker. If I lost, well, I lost—but there was always tomorrow. The same with curling: I was always confident before a game, and my feelings were somehow transmitted to the other players. As a result, our rink always had a good mental attitude going into a competition. Hey, you can't even think of the word 'lose' before you start. Think 'lose'—and you will. We thought 'win'—and we usually did."

MAKING POINTS

When the Richardson Rink was beating the world and winning all those Briers and Scotch Cups, skip Ernie Richardson always used a very simple but very effective game plan to rout the opposition. As he puts it: "We won all our championships by getting rid of every opposition stone in the house. We never took a chance and let their stones stay around. After all, the fewer opposition rocks in the house, the fewer points they could score against us. You might say we were a great take-out team. And now that I think about it, I think we won a lot of games by simply demoralizing the other rinks with our take-outs. They would put a rock in the house, and we would promptly knock it out. After a while the opposition would begin to lose hope."

Although curling is not a contact sport, it is a game of intense physical and mental pressure. The best strategy in a curling match is to apply instant pressure by taking advantage of your team's strengths and your rivals' weaknesses and force them to falter under the strain. A skip's strategy for his team depends upon the particular talents of his players. If they lack take-out power, he should not play a take-out game. But if they have excellent knockout ability, he should certainly use it to the best advantage.

What most curling games come down to, though, is what is known as "last-rock advantage." The side with last-rock advantage is always in the driver's seat. The last rock, after all, can completely cancel out everything the opposition has accomplished in a particular end. In fact, the last rock is so important that (depending on the score) many skips will decide to blank an end by shooting their stone completely through the house rather than win one point and lose that last-rock advantage in the next end. (The winner of one end, of course, plays the first rocks in the next end.)

A hidden psychological advantage with the last rock is the pressure it places on the rival skip. Forced to play a take-out game himself in order to survive, the rival skip may eventually submit to the pressure and miss what looks like an easy take-out of one or more of your rocks. Now you have him in a fix, and you can simply draw into the house and pick up extra points. This kind of pressure can demoralize the opposition and cause them to make more mistakes. And, as Richardson says, "Like all sports, curling comes down to mistakes. The team that makes the fewest mistakes wins. When the Richardson Rink was it its peak, we always made the other team make the mistakes."

93

Although the Richardsons specialized in a knock-'em-out style of attack, there are, of course, other strategies for point-making. Some thoughts about skipping strategy:

1. If at the start of a game you do not have last rock, you as skip should have your lead start off by playing a rock in the center of the house, preferably in front of the tee line, or outside the rings as a guard. Later in the game, if you are ahead by 4 or 5 points, have the lead man stop his rock in front of the tee line so the rival curlers can't freeze to it, or throw it through the house. Richardson used to have his lead throw his rock through the rings when his rink was up 3 or 4 points late in a game. He never wanted too many rocks around the house under such circumstances. By doing that, they put pressure on the other side.

2. Say that you have last-rock advantage in the first end and the rival lead has placed his first rock in the center of the house. Have your lead try to knock him out but still keep his own rock inside. If the rival rock is not in the house, draw to the outside corner of the rings. Ideally, after the first two rocks have been played, only one rock—your lead's second rock—will be in the house.

3. In the first two ends, you as skip should use as much of the rink's surface as possible to learn what the ice is like. Skips who don't do this lose some advantage by not knowing enough about surface conditions. A good skip should know the ice by the beginning of the third end.

4. Say you throw last rock in the first end and there are no rocks in the house. Throw your own rock through the house, blanking the end and therefore holding your last-rock advantage for the next end. Forget that 1 point—believe me, taking it in the first end is bad strategy. A blank end is much better than a 1–0 lead if you have last rock in that first end.

5. When playing draw shots, have your players place their rocks as far apart from each other as possible. This helps prevent the other team from knocking out two of yours with one stone. Also, by doing so, you pressure the opposition into attempting ultradelicate shots—the easiest kind to miss. If they do miss, then

you draw into the middle. Suddenly, you have built up a 3– or 4–point end! And shaken their confidence!

6. When you are down in a game and need points, don't try to take out a rival stone that is only the third or fourth scoring shot in the house, especially when the first and second scoring shots are yours. Instead, draw into the rings as far away from that third or fourth scoring shot as possible.

SKIPPING SIGNALS

Rather than call out instructions to his teammates (a breach of basic curling etiquette), the skip—or the vice-skip—uses a set of signals. While most curling rinks eventually adopt a set of their own, all signals tend to be a slight variation of the signs used decades ago. The following photographs illustrate some of the basic signals.

In-turn. The skip places his broom at the distance needed to make the shot.

95

Extra weight needed. The skip raises his arm above shoulder level and places the broom to show ice needed.

Lighter weight needed. The skip lowers his arm and places the broom to show ice needed.

Corner guard. The skip is asking for a draw around and behind a corner guard. This is for last rock only.

Center guard. The skip is asking for a draw behind a short center guard. He points to the place he wants the curler to place his
rock.

Draw shot. The skip moves his broom in the curving direction he wants the shot to take. He will then pat the ice with the broom to show where he wants the rock to stop.

Take-out shot. The skip indicates a rock; he will then vigorously work his broom back and forth above it to show he wants it removed.

SKIPPING SUGGESTIONS

The following diagrams illustrate some basic placements of rocks under various conditions.

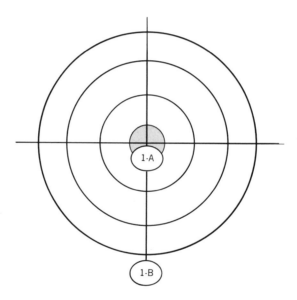

If you do not have last-rock advantage, have your lead place his first rock at 1A or 1B, to block the center. In these positions the stone is good for a guard or a raise.

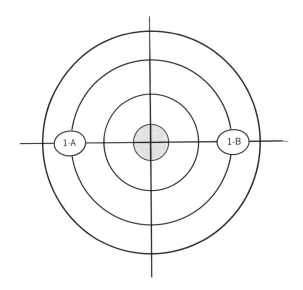

If you have last-rock advantage, place your first rock to either side, at position 1A or 1B, to keep the center open.

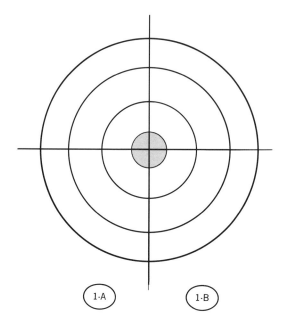

When you are down 2 or more points in the middle ends of a game, place corner guards at position 1A or 1B so that you can draw around them and try to pick up extra points.

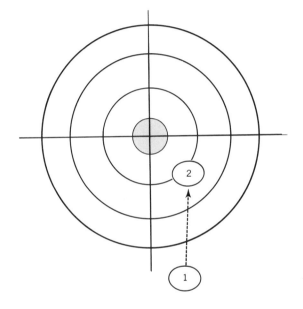

When you have last-rock advantage, a guard in position 1 is good for a raise to position 2.

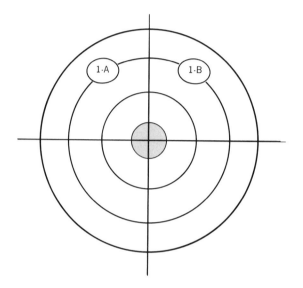

When you are down points with last-rock advantage, draw to opposition rock in position 1A or 1B instead of trying to hit it.

WHY CURL?

Curling is a game that people of all ages can play, and more and more young people are taking up the sport and entering competitions. It offers players the moderate exercise they may otherwise miss during the winter months. Furthermore, it is not a costly activity, because membership in curling clubs is not high and very little equipment is needed. For those who especially enjoy competitive sports, the many bonspiels and club matches offer the challenge of pitting skills and strategy against those of other rinks. Perhaps best of all, it allows people to share in the camaraderie and spirit of good sportsmanship that prevails among curling groups.

Try it . . . you'll like it!